100% UNOFFICIAL

FORTNITE

PRO GUIDE

© 2019 Quarto Publishing Group USA Inc.

First published in 2019 by Dean, an imprint of Egmont UK Limited.
Published in the US by becker&mayer books, an imprint of The Quarto Group, 11120 NE 33rd Place, Suite 201, Bellevue, WA 98004 USA.
www.QuartoKnows.com

becker&mayer! books titles titles are also available at discount for retail, wholesale, promotional, and bulk purchase. For details, contact the Special Sales Manager by email at specialsales@quarto.com or by mail at The Quarto Group, Attn: Special Sales Manager, 100 Cummings Center Suite 265D, Beverly, MA 01915 USA.

19 20 21 22 23 5 4 3 2 1

ISBN: 978-0-7603-6665-3

Library of Congress Cataloging-in-Publication Data available upon request.
Author: Daniel Lipscombe
Design: Joe Bolder
Editorial: Neil Kelly and Jane Riordan
Special thanks to Matthew J. Pratt and Craig Jelley

Printed, manufactured, and assembled in Italy, 06/19

All in-game images: © 2018 Epic Games, Inc.

#330637

FORTNITE

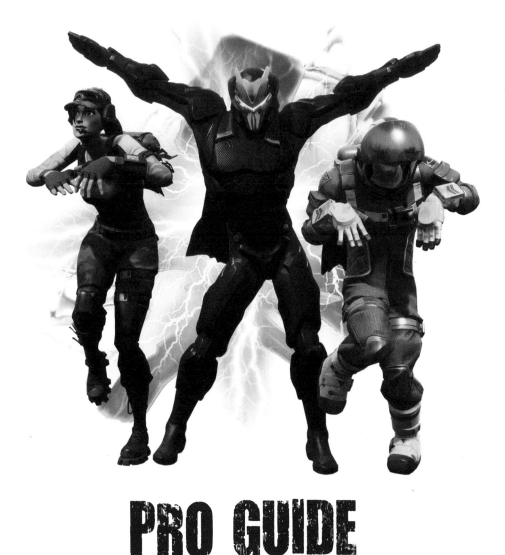

PRO GUIDE

CONTENTS

INTRODUCTION

HELLO AND WELCOME ...

... to this totally unofficial, but totally essential, guide to *Fortnite*, the *Pro Guide*. Since it first came out in September 2017, *Fortnite* has only grown in size. **EVERYBODY** is playing, from your friends in school to chart-topping rock stars, and the game is constantly evolving–rifts opened, a purple cube appeared and got Loot Lake a makeover–then Winter arrived. But it's still the same game under all the fancy new changes; you're still jumping out of the Battle Bus and onto a map filled with 99 other people, hoping to snag that elusive Victory Royale.

Speaking of changes, so much is happening in the game. The map continues to go through **EPIC** shake-ups (see our updated map on page 50); new items and traps are constantly being unleashed and you can now take cute pets into battle with you. In this book we'll take a look at all the new additions as well as give you some must-have tips for building. We'll also hand out some ideas on how to work with your friends as part of a team, and also how to up your game and play more like the **PROS**.

If you want to look great on the battlefield, we've got a showcase of some of the best skins available and plenty of emotes to pair with them. Join us as we explore the world of *Fortnite* and take a look at all the **AMAZING** moments that have occurred so far. It's been a great ride and looks like it can only get better.

So, grab your pickaxe, some materials and your favorite weapon, and tell us where you're dropping.

Let's jump in, and don't forget to thank the bus driver!

The 100% UNOFFICIAL FORTNITE PRO GUIDE team

MOBILE FORTNITE

You might be used to playing *Fortnite* on consoles or PC, but now you can take the fun mobile! Battle Royale was first released to iOS in March 2018, followed by a Nintendo Switch version, before an Android version became available during Season 6, putting *Fortnite* in all our pockets.

NINTENDO SWITCH

Probably the best way to play *Fortnite* in the palm of your hands, the Nintendo Switch gives you a full Battle Royale experience, with all the essential buttons. You can use motion controls if you want, but doing so will make headshots even harder!

While the Switch is completely portable, it doesn't mean you can play ANYWHERE. Most public Wi-Fi hotspots won't support the connection needed to the servers, but if you play at home or at a friend or relative's house, you won't have any issues. You can play in the garden, under your bed, or in your living room. And full voice chat is supported, so maybe don't play on the toilet!

TAKE CONTROL

Forget about winning at first. Spend some time getting used to the controls. The Switch is very slim; holding it is wildly different to a standard controller. Find a comfortable way to hold the console while playing.

ANDROID/iOS

Although it's a lot of fun, playing on a tablet or phone isn't the best way to play *Fortnite*. Playing with a touchscreen is VERY different, so we've put together a few special tips to help score that mobile Victory Royale!

THE SET-UP

- Spend some time learning the controls and playing around with your sensitivity settings. Find what works for you and decide which settings feel natural.

- Use headphones! Playing on a much smaller screen means that sound is all the more important. It doesn't matter what kind of headphones you use, just be aware of footsteps and loud noises.

- Auto-run is very helpful. Usually you'd have to double-tap the screen to run. Get used to always running and it will cut down on the things you need to think about.

7

TIPS FOR BUILDING FAST

Racking up eliminations is fun, but it's no good being a crackshot sniper if you can't build yourself cover or gain higher ground! These tips will help you build faster—leaving you more time to take out your foes and get closer to those all-important Victory Royales.

CHECK YOUR SETTINGS

In the Settings menu, make sure "turbo building" and "auto material change" are switched on. Turbo building enables you to hold the build button to continuously place structures, while auto material change automatically switches you from wood to stone as you run out of materials. It's also good to try different controller sensitivities for your movement. The higher the sensitivity, the faster you can look around, and therefore build more swiftly.

WOOD IS GOOD

Wood is easier to find than stone or metal, and a wooden wall will also build faster than the alternatives. If you need to place a quick ramp or small structure where you can heal, wood is your best bet. Even though a wooden ramp has half the hit points of steel (so can be destroyed more quickly), it can also be replaced faster if you come under fire. Laying down protective wood walls could be the quickest way to save your skin!

PRACTICE

Use Playground mode or quiet moments during gameplay to practice cycling through your build pieces. Learn how quickly structures break down by building one and shooting at it. Practice how long it takes to lay down four walls and a roof, then try and beat your time. Then try editing pieces quickly to add doors and windows. Once it's second nature, you'll be outbuilding everyone!

SMART HARVESTING

We all know that hitting objects with your harvesting tool while moving is the best way to build up resources, but how else can you improve your harvesting technique?

• When swinging your pickaxe at an object, a neon circle will appear.

• Aim your pickaxe at this circle—this will help you break down the object faster.

• You'll still receive the same amount of materials, but you'll harvest them a second or two quicker. This time could be the difference between life and death!

EDIT YOUR BUILD PIECES

While you wait on "Spawn Island" for the match to begin, use any spare time to practice editing your structures. If you have time, edit the pyramid roof into a ramp. This will give you two ramp structures to scroll through, so you can select either one faster. Plus, your new roof-ramp will have the same hit points as a standard ramp.

DON'T PANIC

If you find yourself among the last players, there's a good chance that victory will come down to building. Stay calm and fall back on what you've learned. Think about your options and move through them with care—don't place the wrong structure or get stuck in a corner! Here, solid practice pays off!

OUTBUILD YOUR ENEMY

If you want to outbuild your enemies, you need to think in three dimensions! Try to guess what your foes will do next, as *Fortnite's* final shootouts are often more about building than your skills with guns. Here are some tips on how to win when it's just you—and a bunch of materials—versus your opponents.

MOVE AROUND

Loop around your enemy by building sideways. Whether they're building up or towards you, try to sidestep their movement and get behind them.

If your foe is working on a ramp to get above you, move around to the bottom of their ramp and take them by surprise. The best way to do this is by rapidly laying down floor pieces in front of you as you dash around to their ramp!

BUILD YOUR WALLS

TOP TIP
With skill and a few extra button presses, you can **CONFUSE** others by throwing in the odd steel or brick wall among wooden structures. This can push them to waste ammo.

Being surrounded by your own structures is super-important! Here's why ...

• **You know where your cover is!**

• **You can edit the pieces you have placed.**

If you decide to use precious time and ammo to destroy a wall your enemy has placed, quickly replace it with one of your own. With practice, you can edit the wall into an arch or a half wall, enabling you to fire through it and secure the win.

BUILD UP

High ground is a must in *Fortnite*, whether you're using a shotgun or an assault rifle, so make sure you're moving upwards while also heading towards the enemy. Always try to put a wall down in front of your ramps, whether building up high or on the ground. Doing so means your opponent will need to shoot through the wall before they can damage your ramp.

If you're building a ramp upwards, always build two pieces wide so that your opponent won't know which side you're on. Plus, it gives you somewhere to move to for cover or if one side is being shot at.

TOP TIP
When peeking over the edge of your ramp to shoot or snipe, don't crouch. If your enemy shoots back, you'll have to walk backwards slowly. Instead, stand to peek then crouch behind the edge to take cover.

REBIND YOUR BUTTONS

Don't be scared to change your controls. Many pro players prefer the "Combat Pro" set-up as it allows for faster switching between building and weapons, but you can always change the buttons to suit your own style.

• On a console, you can reposition your building buttons in order to scroll through objects faster.

• On a PC, try a mouse with extra buttons so you can set up your favorite walls to the thumb buttons. You could even move the structures from the Function keys to "C", "V" or "B", as stretching your thumb is quicker and easier than moving your fingers.

FALL BACK

Don't be afraid to back off and build down. Editing a gap in a floor piece and dropping towards the ground will bait your opponent, bringing them down with you. This can easily turn the tables of a fight. If you're falling, keep the flat floor piece handy as you can build it and land on it before taking fall damage.

QUICK BASES

The port-a-fort is perfect when you really need a base quickly, but they're extremely hard to find and you won't often have one available! Here are three bases that are all quick to build, can hold an entire squad, and help you out in a tight spot. Practice building them on your own or with friends and never be caught without cover.

THE HOUSE

The most basic, quick-build structure looks like a house with four walls and a ramp, which can be topped off with more levels or a simple roof. This is an ideal base for quick healing; the build can be completed in just a few seconds.

• Select the wall section and hold the Action button as you turn in a circle. This will make four sturdy walls around you.

• Switch to the ramp and jump into the air as you place it—this will keep you off the ground. If you're surrounded by taller structures or hills, you could add a pointed roof or extra floor above your head to protect you from falling bullets.

• Once you've healed or readjusted to the situation, rather than jumping over the walls, edit the back panel to add a door. This can trick players, who will often approach your structure from the front, not expecting you to appear from around the back.

• Alternatively, you could place yourself under the ramp rather than on top and edit windows into the walls, giving you a hidey-hole to peek out of.

SNIPER TOWER

Unlike the house, the sniper tower is a rectangle rather than a square. This is an ideal base for duos as you can each build one side of the structure and then each defend from either end!

• Start with an oblong made from six walls and position ramps leading up to the narrow ends.

• On top of this rectangular structure, place two floors to enclose and strengthen the base. Repeat the lower layer again.

• This layout will give you some height to see all around you. It enables you to creep up to the edges to scope out opponents, while the inner slopes of the V will allow for cover and healing.

• When the base is finished, it's a good idea to upgrade the materials to stone or metal, which will help protect you from explosions.

TOP TIP
Use the middle of the ramps to store shield potions or bandages, or drop them in your safe hiding space underneath.

THE FUNNEL

Adapted from the house, the funnel looks a little like the port-a-fort. It adds outward ramps to the top of the structure, allowing you to look over the edge and down towards the floor with a clearer view to aim.

• The funnel can be constructed in the same way as the previous builds, but here the idea is to create a cone at the top. Sitting here will allow for cover and a chance to heal, while the ramps let you hang over enemies who approach the bottom of the base.

• Add some doors to the bottom section. Once you're safe inside, you can edit the inside to allow for easy access to the doors. If you're building this base with just two floors, it will allow you to "shotgun drop" from the rim to an enemy below, collect all their lovely loot and scurry back inside!

PRACTICE IN PLAYGROUND

It doesn't matter how good you are with a shotgun or SMG; if you can't build you won't achieve a Victory Royale very often. Muscle memory is the most important skill to train when it comes to building—you should be able to defend yourself or build a base without thinking about it. Training your muscle memory is no easy feat, but Playground mode is a great way to start!

LESSON ONE: "THE 1x1"

The 1x1 is your "go-to" build. It will help with cover and protect you while healing or gaining the high ground. Perfecting the build in a quick time can mean the difference between victory or being sent back to the lobby. Try it out by following these steps. Why not time yourself on a stopwatch and see how fast you can get?

STEP 1 - If you aren't on flat ground, start by placing a floor. If you are, skip to step 2.

STEP 2 - Stand in the middle of your new floor, or on flat ground and select your wall. While holding the Action button, spin in a circle to add four walls.

STEP 3 - Quickly switch to the ramp, jump into the air and place your ramp at the same time. This will place you on top of the ramp and ready for the next step. Move to the top of the ramp before moving on to the next step.

STEP 4 - Place four more walls, jump and place your ramp again. Repeat this until you run out of materials or have built as high as you want to go.

LESSON TWO: "FALLING BUILDS"

Now you have a massive, four-sided tower, it's time to jump off the top and plummet to the ground. Yep, you read that right, we're going to fall from the top. But don't worry, this is to practice the next skill you'll need: building while falling.

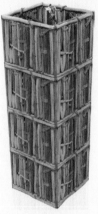

STEP 1 - Jump off the tower.

STEP 2 - You'll want to select a building structure, either a flat floor or ramp works best. As you're falling, guide yourself close to the walls of the tower.

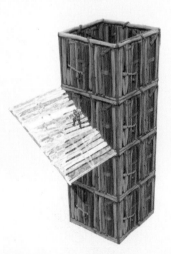

STEP 3 - Aim towards the wall slightly and tap the Action button to build your floor or ramp. Rather than splat on the ground you'll find yourself standing safely on your new structure.

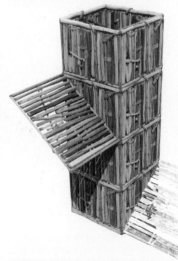

STEP 4 - Keep going until you reach the ground without losing any health.

LESSON THREE: "AGGRESSIVE RAMPS"

Ramps are the perfect way to gain the high ground on your enemy. Gather some materials and find yourself a clear space on the map, preferably next to a mountain, which we'll use as our target point. Aim your ramps at the top of the mountain.

STEP 1 - Place a ramp in front of you and begin walking upwards. Once you've nailed the technique you can practice building while sprinting.

STEP 2 - While your ramp is building and you're moving forward, switch to a wall and place it in front of you at the tip of the slope. The wall will protect your ramp from attack.

STEP 3 - Once you've done this a few times, add a floor into the mix. The floor will need to cover the underside of your ramp, adding another layer of protection. Try making the ramp first, then add the floor, then build the wall.

STEP 4 - Now try the previous steps again, but with two ramps side-by-side.

LESSON FOUR: "EDITING AND LAYERING"

Take a look at your creations. You'll have a huge tower and several ramps standing in front of you. Now it's time to edit those awesome structures, adding in doors, windows and arches. Editing as you move can save your skin, give you time to heal and get back into the fight.

EDIT 1 - While building a long ramp upwards, try adding a floor above you. Once the floor is placed, edit the two squares on one side to convert it into a half floor–the new gap will allow you to continue climbing up as well as offer overhead cover as you get closer to your target.

EDIT 2 - Stand sideways on to the wall and build a ramp, ready to climb. Before you begin moving, place another ramp directly above the one you plan to walk on. Auto building will allow you to move your aim up and down, adding to both ramps as you go!

DID YOU KNOW?

This advanced technique is known as "Scissor Stairs" and is best done against a cliff face or large wall as it gets you to high points quickly, but with cover from above and below.

EDIT 3 - The "roof rush" is similar to placing ramps and takes some quick switching skills. It helps you to hold the high ground, and is useful for running out of the storm while keeping cover. Head to the top of a tower or mountain and place a floor. As you're running out onto the floor, put down a pyramid roof. Place this combo of structures ahead of you as you run, so that anyone below you will have to shoot through the floor before they can shoot the pyramid. This gives you vital seconds to escape!

CREATIVE MODE

If you've ever imagined developing your own *Fortnite* Battle Royale island, then Creative Mode is well worth trying. Start Creative Mode and you'll skydive onto your very own island, a blank slate for you to do whatever you want with ... literally. The options available to you here are as good as infinite, so we've put together the following tips to help you be a creative master!

GETTING STARTED

If it's your first time playing in Creative Mode then you'll want to jump onto a fresh new island and experiment as much as possible. You're given an allocation of four blank islands to build on and you can dip in and out of them, so don't worry if one turns out imperfect.

Start by familiarizing yourself with some of the new options you have at your disposal. Laying down some prefabricated buildings or a fleet of vehicles is totally new and will take some getting used to. Once you know your way around the new controls, decide on a project and start constructing. The new mobile phone in your inventory allows you to manipulate any item already on your island.

SQUAD

Building alone is fun but building with your squad is fast! Invite your online crew to your map—or join theirs—and combine your skills and manpower to achieve more in less time. Devise and communicate a plan through your headsets and then get to work making it a reality!

With so many Creative Mode options available to you, you can have real fun creating your islands as a team and enjoying them together. If you built a straight-up Battle Royale island then invite another squad to take you on, or if you built a racetrack with daredevil jumps and insane loops then start your engines and get racing.

RESOURCEFUL

Clicking on your inventory will open up a library stacked with options. Prefabs, devices, weapons, consumables, and chests have all have tabs containing loads of options for your island. From placing a clocktower in the centre of a small city, to littering it with rocket launchers—the choice is yours! As well as all these ready-made elements, you also have unlimited resources, so you can build, build, build with as much wood, stone or metal as you want! This extra practice, with no one shooting at you, will help make you a faster and smarter builder later, when you're in the heat of battle.

BLOCK PARTY

What's the point in spending lots of time on something if you're not going to show it off? Once you've created something you're truly happy with then get sharing. Anyone can visit your island to check out your creation, whether you've made a mad racetrack or booby-trapped map for some surprise Battle Royale action! Head to Epic's website for more info on sharing—if your island meets their specifications and they like the look of it then you could see your island displayed in Battle Royale's The Block!

TOP TIP
Practice makes perfect. Use the prefab structures to replicate difficult situations you've found yourself in before and practice getting out of them, both quickly and easily.

PRO PICK-UPS

We've watched hours of *Fortnite* online and played hundreds of games, looking at which weapons and items the pros like to use. These weapons and items are a few that most pro players tend to look for or favor. Whether you want to destroy enemies or structures or maybe move around faster and smarter, the pros can teach you all you need to know.

WEAPONS

ASSAULT RIFLE

The assault rifle comes in all rarities, but the Rare (blue) rifle can be found often and packs a punch. With a quick reload speed and plenty of damage, this rifle is a must-have. When it comes to spraying bullets, the DPS here can cause real trouble for your enemy.

COMPACT SMG

The compact SMG is one of the harder guns to find and doesn't work brilliantly at distance. However, one of these in close quarters, like a room in a building, will take out your enemy before they even know what hit them. Huge DPS fired over short bursts make this gun one to have.

SUPPRESSED PISTOL

This pistol isn't the best for damage, but you can stay quiet while using it. Firing the suppressed pistol creates very little noise, allowing you to sneak around! Useless against structures, it's best used for a surprise attack to be followed up with a shotgun.

HEAVY SHOTGUN

This absolute monster is sometimes overlooked because it requires some mastering. But once you can wield it confidently and hit the target, the damage it can dish out is seriously devastating. If you can nail a headshot with this then you can consider yourself a pro!

PUMP SHOTGUN

The most common shotgun on the map, this one is better for those who struggle a little to aim up-close. You can let off five shots in a quick burst and while the damage is much lower than the heavy shotgun, it can throw off your enemy and force them into changing their tactics.

HEAVY SNIPER RIFLE

There are a few sniper rifles in *Fortnite* and many are great for pinning down your enemy. But this is your best choice if you want to take them out in one clean shot. The damage on the Legendary drop is over 150 and if you can steady your hand for a headshot, it'll be game over!

ROCKET LAUNCHER

It's obvious that rockets do damage and even though they're great for taking out opponents, you have to factor in the distance and speed of the rocket. They're best used to break down bases. The Legendary rocket launcher has a structure damage stat of over 400! **BOOM!**

ITEMS

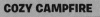

GRAPPLER

Although only available now in Playground and Creative, the grappler is a handy item. With some practice, you can use it to climb the outside of tall bases, jump over large gaps or move across ground faster. Be careful: it only holds ten uses, but if used well you'll be able to surprise your enemy as you fly through the air.

COZY CAMPFIRE

While not the best item for quick healing in *Fortnite*, the cozy campfire is great for your team to recharge after a tough fight. As a long fight comes to an end and most of your team are on low health, build a 1x1 and drop a campfire in the middle for everyone to gather around. The campfire can heal up to 50 points and does so at 2 HP per second. Great for Squads matches!

CHUG JUG

The ultimate in shields and healing! You can only carry one of these at a time and they take 15 seconds to use, but they can change a match. If you're low on health and shields, find somewhere to take cover and chug this jug to fill both to maximum. They're very rare, so don't hold onto it "just in case"–be tactical.

TOP TIP
Chug Jugs are probably the most powerful healing item in the game, so if you have one and your shields and health are full, share with your squad to ensure you're all in the best condition.

SPECIALS AND TRAPS

Using special build items such as traps can give you a slight advantage over your opponents. They can be used to move faster across distance or to protect your bases. On their own they can already cause trouble, but combining them can be devastating!

RETRACTABLE FLOOR SPIKE

Trap: Using the spike trap can get you a few eliminations here and there. Always put your trap onto ceilings or walls, never the floor. A cautious player will always spot a trap on the floor, but by placing it above them you can take them by **SURPRISE.** Bait your traps by placing them just inside an unopened door, or near to unopened chests or Llamas, leading players towards your nasty little surprise. They simply won't see it coming!

Trick: If you find more than one spike trap and your building skills are good enough (this will take lots of practice), you can "trap box" someone. You need to be fast—stand above where your enemy will walk and begin laying the traps as they walk past you. Stealth is key here as it won't work if they hear you. Place a spike trap onto the wall next to your foe; this will panic them and cause 75 damage. Swiftly place another trap on the opposite wall, ceiling or both to contain them inside a spike trap "box".

LAUNCH PAD

Trap: The launch pad isn't a standard trap, but it can be used to confuse your enemy. Make them think you've bounced out of the area when in fact you've moved behind them! If someone is chasing you, quickly lay a flat floor and launch pad in order to spring upwards and glide off. They'll think that you're making a getaway, but if you loop around behind them you can take them out with a shotgun blast–**BOOM!** Launch pads can be used by anyone; if your foe jumps on your pad, stand back and, if you're a serious pro, maybe even snipe them out of the air!

Trick: Always use your launch pads at height to make the most of the movement. If the pad's low to the ground, you'll need to be moving fast to gain enough height to change position or regroup. Use your launch pad to boost you into the air and enable you to soar far away to safety on your glider.

CHILLER TRAP

Trap: Chiller traps don't hold people in place, but they are perfect for sliding opponents into spike traps or boosting them off a high drop. If you're being chased towards the end of a game, while building up high, dropping a chiller can see your enemy lose control of their movement. Sadly, these traps have been vaulted from the main game but you can still have fun with them in Playground.

Trick: Want to move faster? Place a chiller trap on a downward-sloping ramp and begin running down. Your feet will **FREEZE,** and you'll move faster than the standard run. Wanna go even faster? Throw a shockwave grenade towards your feet as you run; this will explode just behind you and you'll outrun anyone or anything around you.

EMOTES: EXPRESS YOURSELF!

Emotes are a huge part of *Fortnite*. Everybody's doing the Floss and you'll even see it on TV dancing competitions! Whether you're celebrating a win or taunting a foe, there's always an emote to fit. With so many emotes available to express yourself, here's our guide to some of the very best.

SHOWSTOPPER

You've just found your favorite Epic gun. It's scored you wins in the past, and maybe it's been a few games since you last saw it. You want to dance with joy, so unleashing the wild arm-waving of Showstopper is a sure-fire way to  show your excitement! Your avatar swings their arms from side to side then spins them both in the air.

DANCE MOVES

As the starting emote, Dance Moves is often overlooked as a worthy dance to use—most people will think you're a noob. However, there's something timeless about the clap-happy, foot-shuffling of Dance Moves that makes  it perfect to celebrate a knock down, especially when you reach the smug arm-cross at the end.

LIVING LARGE

Instead of leaping into the air in celebration, why not just shimmy from side to side, palms up? This suggests it's all in a day's work for you to drop from the Battle Bus and dominate the battlefield. Imagine taking out your last

opponent with a long-range sniper shot, or outbuilding an enemy, ending in the perfect shotgun win ... mission accomplished!

ORANGE JUSTICE

Make sure you limber up for this move. Throw caution to the wind and spin your arms around, getting lower as you go, and add in a  few claps for good measure. Orange Justice may make you look crazy, but you'll be much harder to hit with such frantic movements. It could really irritate snipers if you're taunting from a distance.

TAKE THE ELF

Shut down your enemy in style with this seasonal spin on the popular Take The L emote. Great for a little bit of mischief making, you can outplay the opponent, throwing up some cover  at just the right moment before taking them out. Take The Elf is the perfect way to let an enemy know they lost, no matter the time of year.

GET FUNKY

Reserved for the flyest Fortniters out there, Get Funky is one of those emotes that really oozes coolness. It's all about the arms! The hip-swishing, air-grabbing,  rodeo-riding combo will definitely make you stand out from the crowd, and it pairs perfectly with any outfit—the crazier the outfit, the cooler it gets ... Trust us.

BEST MATES

The perfect emote to use in conjunction with your Duos partner, Best Mates is a blend of frantic jogging on the spot and rhythmic arm-dangling. Its comedic effect multiplies with every person that uses it, so make sure you gather everyone in your squad to set up an ultra-emote show.

FLOSS

This iconic move has grown so big that you see it everywhere in the real world—it's a true phenomenon, for sure. It requires speed, intense coordination, straight legs and loose arms to pull off, but there's nothing more irritating to a recently knocked-down enemy than seeing those arms swinging from side to side at lightning speed.

INFINITE DAB

An upgraded version of the legendary Dab, which won't quit until you do. Nothing will rub salt in the wound of a recently picked-off enemy than seeing you dabbing incessantly over their loot. Use it sparingly though—all that twisting and nodding your head could really cause you an injury!

SKINS: LOOKING COOL!

Fortnite is all about fighting, building and showing off! Choosing a cool skin makes you stand out on the battlefield, and, as with the emotes, they're a major part of the game. With loads of great skins to choose from, there's something to suit everyone's style! Here are some of our favorites ...

NITELITE

You'll never be afraid of the dark again, wearing this neon glow skin! We can't decide if this skin is better suited for Halloween or for throwing some amazing emote shapes at a disco! One thing's for sure, there's nothing funkier than dropping into the battle with Nitelite's Glow Rider glider!

HAY MAN

Normally, scarecrows are used out in the fields to keep birds away from crops, but this one is more likely to help keep opponents away from you! Hay Man may look like it was made from some loose materials hanging in Fatal Fields, but that just makes it supernaturally scary on the battlefield!

GUAN-YU

This regal skin will give you the look of a legendary warrior, so don't blow it by making silly mistakes, or camping in the corner like a coward! This skin lets people know you're in it to win it, so glide down on the Divine Dragon glider and get chasing that victory!

RAVAGE

Looking the business on the battlefield doesn't get much darker than this. If your game revolves around stealth, with plucky long shots and unexpected takedowns—not to mention scaring the wits out of other players—then you'll like Ravage. This skin is seriously grim!

DJ YONDER

What do you get when you mix a robotic llama helmet with a disco ball? We never thought we'd ask that question but we **LOVE** the answer. This funkadelic destroyer proves you don't need boogie bombs to distract your enemies while you spin your way to victory!

SGT. WINTER

You'll have no reason to fear the winter weather again once you're wearing this super-tough skin. You can be sure players will fear seeing you marching across the map because Sgt. Winter means business. Until his final stage, that is. Then he starts messing about in a llama mask!

DANTE

Even being dead hasn't stopped Dante from chasing the taste of Victory Royale. Sure, he's a bit of a show-off (his pickaxe is a sweet guitar called the Six String Striker!) but you're always going to get a good show when this guy is performing, especially after dark, when he really comes alive!

DUSK

This pale-skinned power player is especially haunting at night. Her eerie red eyes and vampiric style make her a menacing sight on the island. So when the moon comes out you'd better watch out— unless you're using this skin, in which case sit back and enjoy the horror show!

SUMMIT STRIKER

If reaching the top is your game, then this is the skin for you. With Summit Striker you'll look well at home on top of the game's many mountains. It looks the part on any terrain and you'll be playing with a smile because the Summit Striker pack is cheap and comes with 600 V-Bucks. Get involved!

LYNX

When Season 7 landed, Lynx was one of several new skins that came to play in the snow. At stage 1 she's pretty chill and friendly, but by stage 3 she's kitted out in a terrifying cyber suit! She may not give you nine lives, but she will terrify your opponents into submission.

TAKE YOUR PET TO WORK

The pets might seem like extra, fancy back bling, but they add a lot of character to your player. Not only are they crazy cute, but they react to what happens around you! Pets launched in Season 6 and began with only three that could be unlocked through the Battle Pass; it all started with a dog, a dragon, and a chameleon. While they don't change any mechanics in the game, they're great company as you venture out into battle.

BONESY

Bonesy the dog starts off in an orange color, but can soon be changed to white and brown through higher tiers. With big, bright eyes and a little neck scarf, Bonesy sits in your backpack and will look fierce when you take aim at an enemy, or smile if you nab the Victory Royale. This lively puppy is perfect for active players because, even though he just wants to run around and play, he's such a good boy really!

CAMO

Camo the chameleon is so cute! Camo reacts much like Bonesy-peering over your shoulder as you look down the rifle scope-but of course, as a chameleon, Camo can change color and does so to reflect the rarity of any item you collect. Watch as Camo latches onto your back bling with its tail as your drop from the bus, or dances and claps when things are going well on the battlefield.

SCALES

Scales the dragon tries so very hard to look as scary as possible. With big pointy teeth and angry eyes, Scales is trying to watch your back, but a tiny dragon like this can only be lovable. Scales comes in three colors, starting with blue. Pink and black can also be unlocked. Remember, those wings are only for show and Scales can't help you if you fall from a great height!

MERRY MUNCHKIN

This limited-edition gingerbread pet was only available by completing the 14 Days of *Fortnite* event! *Fortnite* pets don't get much sweeter than this.

HAMIREZ

Don't let her small size fool you-this pet wheel-y wants to be your Battle Royale companion and with her own wheel and feeder she's ready to go!

REMUS

Watch out if you want to pet this cool character-it's anything but tame! Tier 93 of Season 7's Battle Pass rewarded you with a slick ice version.

LTM-LIMITED TIME MODES

Fortnite is famous for its Battle Royale mode, but there's more to the game than Solo, Duos, and Squads. Epic recently began introducing Limited Time Modes with the 50v50 match type. There have been over 20 LTMs since the launch of 50v50, and each one experiments with new ways to play. Here's a look at some of the most fun modes so far!

50v50

Why not start with the original LTM—the one that kicked it all off. 50v50 takes two massive squads of fifty players, each with their own Battle Bus and pits them against each other. The map is also split into two halves—crossing the line will make it more likely you'll run into the opposing team—giving each team ten minutes to **LOOT** the map before the storm begins to close in. This mode makes the final fight incredibly tense and exciting because practically everyone is decked out with great weapons and they all pour into the circle, building huge bases to take down!

SNIPER SHOOTOUT

Sniper Shootout doesn't shake up the usual gameplay that much, but it does force you to play in a very different and slower way. Limiting the weapons on the map to just sniper rifles and sometimes crossbows, each match is a true battle of wits. No one can run around with a minigun so battles are slower-paced. While you may not be all that great with scoped weapons, this LTM will give you a chance to practice, as long as you don't mind getting taken out by sharpshooters across the map! It's a tough, but very rewarding mode to play.

ONE SHOT

If you've ever fancied a bit of moon walking, then this is the LTM for you. With its low gravity setting you'll find yourself slowly bouncing around the map. It may sound chilled but the storm wait time has been greatly reduced in all phases of the game, so watch out. It's also worth noting that pretty much the only weapons in this mode are hunting rifles and sniper rifles. Players will spawn with 50 health and can only heal if they find bandages as they are the only healing item. There are also no shields in this mode. So stay safe, enjoy those high jumps and aim well - One Shot is out of this world!

HIGH EXPLOSIVES

Similar to Sniper Shootout, High Explosives removes all weapons except those that go **BOOM.** Rockets, grenades, and guided missiles are the highlights as everything on the map explodes while players try to take each other out in the most extravagant way. It's worth noting that the ammo and material spawn rates are greater, encouraging you to keep building structures for friends and enemies alike to blow up. Where Sniper Shootout was slower-paced, High Explosives flips that and causes nothing but pure **CHAOS.**

FIND YOUR STYLE

You may find some game types more fun, or discover that particular modes suit your style of play more than others. If you're just starting out with *Fortnite* then we suggest trying out all the basic modes until you find the one that's most fun for you!

BLITZ

You'd better move fast; the storm starts closing in from the moment you land on the map. Blitz is all about **SPEED,** as the maximum match length is only fifteen minutes. All spawn rates are increased and the gaps between the storm closing in are reduced. To play Blitz, you need to stay on your toes, keep moving, and play aggressively. There's no time for building bases or camping with a sniper rifle, but Epic still wants those tremendous build-offs so all materials are doubled—make sure you've practiced your ramp rushing!

SOLID GOLD

Who wants green or blue weapon drops nowadays? Solid Gold is all about those Legendary drops. The map and storm haven't changed, but now every chest contains a golden weapon. Floor drops will see more hand cannons and suppressed pistols instead of assault or sniper rifles and chests will likely cough up assault rifles or miniguns, but no pistols at all. There's an increased spawn rate for shield potions and chug jugs and all those lovely materials will be bumped up too. This mode is great for creating **HECTIC** moments and perfect for showing off your skills.

LEGENDARY FEEL!

Some game modes, like Solid Gold, are great for experiencing the perks of Legendary weapons, but don't get too familiar with them. When the game mode ends and you're back using regular weapons, they won't be as powerful and you could get caught out.

GETAWAY

One very limited mode is Getaway, which brings more of an objective-based concept to the battlefield compared to all-out elimination. The goal is to find a jewel and drop it off at a getaway van. Obviously, carrying the jewel makes you a target so working together is paramount to scoring the Victory Royale. With four jewels and four vans, winning can occur at any time. Resources are increased by 50% and only rare or better weapons drop. This mode completely shakes up the game and will force you to think differently as you explore and play.

SCORE ROYALE

What if your eliminations and the chests you opened allowed you to score points and those points were totalled up across a team? This is exactly what Score Royale is. At the start of the match, the storm moves slowly but speeds up as the game progresses. This makes for some epic, early looting, and serious **ACTION** later on! You can score 50 points for opening a llama, 100 for eliminating an enemy, and there are gold, silver and bronze coins which also boost your tally. Once the point threshold has been passed, that team wins.

CHALLENGE ACCEPTED?

Challenges are great for increasing your levels, but as they can often be a distraction from achieving Battle Royale success! However, some game modes are suited to challenges more than others—when one is, jump in and make the most of it.

WHAT'S YOUR ROLE?

How you play *Fortnite* will be different from how your friends play but each of you can complement the other by learning what your strengths are. Maybe you like to scope out the map for advantages? Or perhaps you like to find the best weapon and start taking out the other teams. You might even be the one who holds onto the medkits and bandages. What role should you fill?

ASSAULT

This role tends to go to those who have no fear in close-range shotgun battles, or the member who can pin down an enemy with an assault rifle. You'll need to enter buildings first to check if the coast is clear and will be the first to give chase when the enemy is on the run. This role requires the best loot in order to carry out your attacks.

TIPS

TIP 1 - While you might want to rely on your medic, make sure you have some shield potions and a few bandages—you're going to get shot at, a lot. Practice lining up your shots as you jump around, try to confuse your opponent.

TIP 2 - Listen to your team. There's no point bursting into a building if a teammate has seen someone else enter a side door. Perhaps combine with another member and approach a situation from two sides at once.

TIP 3 - Be aware. Listen out for footsteps or doors being used around you. Always ask your team where they are and what they see. Build a picture in your mind of the area.

MEDIC

Being the medic of your team is risky as it will limit the number of weapons you can carry in order to hold loads of healing items. But it is very rewarding when a teammate is down, and you can swoop in to rescue them. Keep your shields full at all times, in order to soak up damage while healing others.

TIPS

TIP 1 – Make sure to focus on bandages, medkits, and keep some shield potions handy. Leave the best guns for your squad but keep an assault rifle or SMG in order to lay down some cover fire when it's needed.

TIP 2 – You'll need some building materials to construct walls around a fallen friend, so practice setting up small bases with speed. Four walls will often be enough, but experiment with ramps and pyramids. Find what works for you.

TIP 3 – Don't wander off. Stick close to your squad so that you can drop items as they need them or dash in to revive somebody. Call out if you are running low on supplies, then your team can go looting with you.

SUPPORT

To play the role of support, you'll need to be good at everything. You'll spend time building towers to scout the area for enemies, but also use a sniper rifle to take out people from a distance when they're sneaking up on teammates. Practice building towers quickly, so you can gain the high ground, when needed.

TIPS

TIP 1 – It's helpful to have a rocket launcher, if you can loot one, then you can fire into a base before your team swarms the enemy. Explosions also create great distractions. Fire to one side while your team approaches from another.

TIP 2 – As a supporting member of the team, you need to think about how you can help situations; maybe using grenades to cause chaos or peppering the area with fire to keep enemies in place. Use your shots to guide the enemy towards where your team lay in wait.

TIP 3 – You'll need a rifle. Looking down its sight is helpful for letting your team know where enemies are, and what weapon they're using, allowing them to adjust their own immediate tactics!

WHAT NOT TO DO

There are a lot of little mistakes we make when learning the ropes of *Fortnite*. Some can be quite obvious, but plenty will go unnoticed. On these pages we've pointed out some of the biggest errors that new players make—so you won't!

STAIRWAY TO HEAVEN

The most common mistake that all new players make is building ramps straight up with no protection or awareness of players in the area. Whether it be a need to scout the area, chase an enemy, or pursue a challenge, so many people build ramps only to reach the top and have another player blast the bottom section. Being eliminated on the battlefield by a clever shotgun drop or long-range shot is fine, but falling to your doom from height will leave you feeling salty. By cutting out these silly, unnecessary eliminations you're far more likely to progress further in every match you play.

DISTRACTIONS

Don't always chase challenges. Part of the fun of the *Fortnite* Battle Pass is the weekly challenges, but if you get too wrapped up in dancing at certain points or shooting clay pigeons, you're likely to be **TAKEN OUT**. If you want to work on challenges, then drop into the less populated areas and play around for the first couple of minutes of the match. These challenges will be completed over time and your focus should be on gathering materials and getting the upper hand for the endgame.

GOING IN UNPREPARED

Never go into a fight unprepared, especially if it's likely to end in a build-off. You'll obviously need ammo for whichever gun you favor, but gathering materials is just as important. Without wood or stone, you will lose mobility and cover when needed the most. You must always go into a fight thinking that it will end in sprawling structures. Unless you're building or shooting, your pickaxe should be equipped to mine away at any and all resources.

EXPOSURE

Often players will neglect to protect themselves from others creeping up on them or attacking from the sides (outflanking). Of course, you don't want to box yourself up because you won't be able to see who might be approaching from any direction. If you've practiced enough then customizing your builds won't take long. You can add window openings to your walls or use half-wall structures for that much-needed cover. You'll find they're perfect for ducking behind, taking a quick break and then using a new shield potion or reloading your weapons.

GOING IT ALONE

Try to pair up with a friend or join a group when seeking out those special challenges. Take it in turns to perform the action while the other players watch your back!

CROWD CONTROL

All those tall buildings or grouped structures are very tempting to new players. Surely the rooms will be bursting with chests holding promise of legendary loot. Areas such as Tilted Towers and Retail Row are like **BAITED TRAPS** for experienced players or campers who wait for noobs to wander in. Dropping into these areas requires much more luck than skill—if you don't drop on a chest or at least a green gun, you're as good as dead. If you insist on dropping here, watch where other players are gliding to and keep an eye out for weapons in the open that will give you a quick pick-up.

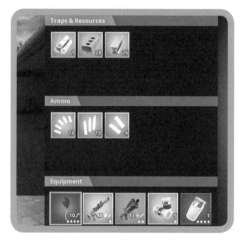

MESSY INVENTORY

Always keep a tidy inventory. If you favor using certain weapons then keep them in the same slots at the start of your hotbar. Position bandages and shields at the end of your hotbar, and when trouble starts, your brain will instantly know where to grab these vital healing items. Don't pick up items "just in case"—if you don't normally use Boogie bombs, then leave them behind and keep that slot for something more important or useful. It's easy to get carried away picking up everything, especially if it's a rare item.

LEGENDARY

Legendary doesn't always mean better. If you watch pros playing online, you'll sometimes see them favor a lower tier weapon. While these may pack less punch they can sometimes handle recoil or range a little better than their orange cousins.

LOOT HUNGRY

This common mistake goes hand in hand with a messy inventory. So many players will take out an enemy before running full speed into the glorious pile of loot that awaits them. However, doing this is a good way to be taken out by someone on the edge of the battle.

Many fights are incredibly **LOUD** and will attract more confident players to take you—or whoever you're fighting—out, and to collect any dropped loot. If you manage to gain a win over someone else, make sure to place some quick cover before collecting your goodies and prioritize getting your health as full as possible.

LISTEN OR BE AWARE

Fortnite focuses heavily on hearing what other players are doing around you. Footsteps are pronounced, and explosions and gunshots give away the direction of battle. If you can hear someone near you, then you better believe they can hear you too. It's easy to get eager and run towards the sound of someone harvesting materials inside a house, but as soon as they hear you they'll get ready with a shotgun for the moment you appear. Your best choice in this close-quarters situation is to find a corner and stand still—eventually, their own impatience will lead them to you.

DID YOU KNOW?

If you are hard of hearing, Epic have a perfect option which can be activated to turn sound effects into an on-screen visual, alerting you to the direction of nearby action.

45

TEAMWORK TIPS

Once you and your friends have all chosen a role to play or found a position you feel comfortable with, it's time to get into Squads and get that Victory Royale! Working as a team can be difficult though. You all have to work together and think in similar ways. These tips should help you out!

MOVE AND DROP TOGETHER

This is such a simple tip but use the opening time on the starting island to discuss where you want to drop. If you want to play **AGGRESSIVELY** you'll need to drop early, so there's no point in waiting until you're on the bus. Decide early and when you hit the ground, stick together. For a team of four people, avoiding places like Tilted Towers is best because you could end up getting in each other's way. Lazy Links, Happy Hamlet, and Lonely Lodge are reasonably open, but also give your team a chance to keep an eye on each other.

TOP TIP
Learn to outflank. Outflanking is a skill used by armies across the world whereby your squad splits in half and moves around the enemy to attack from two sides. This is an ideal tactic for pinning down an enemy before going in for the win.

EMOTING

Playing with a microphone is always best, but sometimes you just can't turn it on for whatever reason. This is where emotes work well, particularly "Stop", "Go! Go! Go!" or "Thumbs Up" and "Thumbs Down". Use these if you desperately need to signal your team but don't have a working microphone. You may still be hearing them talk and can react to what they say.

COMMUNICATE

Tell each other what you're finding inside chests or on the floor. With time, you'll get to know who prefers what weapon or who favors the rocket launcher over grenades. If you hear footsteps then say so, don't just run off without backup. Two guns are always better than one so, when all that loot drops, make sure that you're sharing-particularly with healing items and ammo. After a fight, take a little time to ask who needs healing or discuss where you'd like to move to. Playing as a unit is the only way to score those wins and keep having fun.

LEARN COORDINATES AND CALL-OUTS

The compass at the top of the screen should be your best friend when working as a team. Not only can you use it to give a direction to your squad without opening the map, but you can use the number coordinates to point out where enemies might be. If you're facing south east for example and see an enemy dash across the map, you can call out "120" to your team, advising them all at once where there is enemy movement.

ENCOURAGE EACH OTHER

Always congratulate a teammate on a good choice of tactic or a win in a fight. It's so important to let each other know that they're a vital part of the team. **CELEBRATE** the highlights and lean on each other if you lose—the best teams in the world are the best because they support each other. You won't win together if you don't learn to lose together too. When the match ends, talk about what went well and share your favorite moments. It is a game after all and games are meant to be fun. So enjoy it!

TOP TIP
Watch your building and don't build on top of each other. Work together to form a defensive base but keep a little distance between you if you're ramp rushing or building high ground.

BENDING THE RULES

Gamers will always try to bend the rules of a game, looking for new ways to play. It's part of the fun! Trying to find silly tricks or wacky eliminations will always be a big part of *Fortnite* and the internet is filled with people doing crazy stuff. Thankfully Epic Games always enjoy seeing how the community reacts to new additions or glitches, so many of them stay in the game.

ROCKET RIDING

Rocket riding started over Halloween 2017 when the rockets became jack-o'-lanterns. Players suddenly noticed that if a rocket was fired towards the feet of a teammate, the ally would travel with the rocket. This brought about lots of videos of people escaping the storm or even landing a headshot with a sniper rifle ... from the rocket! At first you needed a ramp to get the right height but now it's possible by timing a good jump. A rocket-riding emote was added soon after and some streamers even managed to pull off the move with the grenade launcher too!

GRAPPLE GUN & RIFT IN PLAYGROUND

The grapple gun already allows for amazing movement. You can use it to reach higher areas with speed, or even travel over small gaps with long drops underneath. The grapple gun uses a suction cup to attach to a surface and then pulls you towards it quickly. Some players have found that if you do this and slingshot yourself into a rift you'll redeploy much faster, gain a little extra height when exiting the rift and confuse any friends nearby. Teaming the grapple with a rift-to-go is very difficult, but with practice, could be possible.

BOUNCE PAD & CHILLERS IN PLAYGROUND

As soon as the chiller trap was released, players began to look for interesting ways to use it. It started with many heading into Playground mode and lining up huge chains of the traps. Doing this, players managed to create ice rinks! Moving was made a little harder, but after time it was easy to control the slide. When combined with a bounce pad, it would give players a burst of speed. Unlike other items, whose tricks could be difficult to pull off, ice movement is incredibly easy. Just set up a ramp with a bounce pad on it and a chiller trap in front of it and skate away from danger!

OUTLANDISH BUILDS IN PLAYGROUND

Not exactly bending the rules, but Playground doesn't just allow for practice, but also for building **HUGE** castles, statues, and race tracks! If you have an idea for something to build, it's probably possible. Grab your friends and a bunch of materials and start building. By editing structure pieces, you have a very deep set of tools to create with. But remember, you only have an hour! Make sure everyone knows what they're doing and don't forget to take a screenshot to show off your creation after!

THE MAP

The *Fortnite* map has changed a lot since the game first came out. Some areas have seen more change than others for better or worse—Kevin the cube created havoc! Below, we've looked at some of the most important changes.

WAILING WOODS

Wailing Woods is getting a lot more detail thanks to new buildings. Extra cabins have appeared throughout the woods and a new underground bunker has been constructed where someone is doing experiments with rifts!

TILTED TOWERS

Tilted Towers continues to change. Buildings wrecked by the comet were rebuilt only to be wrecked again by the wandering cube. It remains a very built-up area, so there's always something new cropping up here—and loads of dangerous opponents.

LOOT LAKE

Briefly known as Leaky Lake, its middle island lifted into the air on a whirlwind. You could use the winds to redeploy with your glider, or swoop up to the loot-filled island itself!

HAUNTED HILLS

Haunted Hills became a huge feature for Halloween as a haunted castle was constructed on the peak. With lots of towers for sniping and plenty of chests, it became a popular spot to drop.

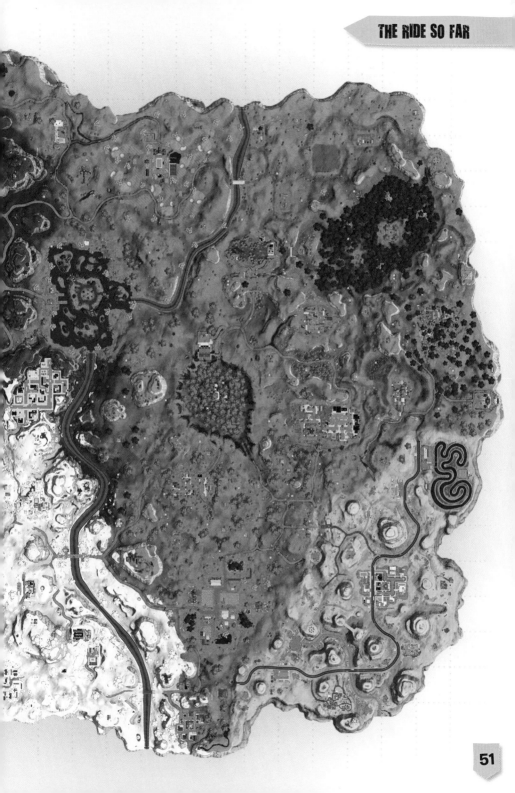

TEN EPIC MOMENTS

Fortnite has created some great moments. Many of them have changed the map or the way we play. Some brought in millions of players to work together, whereas others were confusing. The exciting thing is that the game is constantly evolving and introducing awesome changes. We've picked out ten of the biggest moments in the life of *Fortnite* ... so far!

BATTLE PASS

The introduction of the Battle Pass was a huge shift for *Fortnite*. The pass brought loads of challenges for you and your mates, it rewarded you with XP boosts, new skins and spray tags plus odd bundles of V-Bucks. Sure, it cost you (or your parents) a bit of money, but the value was enormous. The Battle Pass constantly brings new life to the game, particularly around big celebrations like the first birthday event. There is always a new skin to chase and show off while playing. While the challenges can sometimes be a bit of a distraction, we loved dancing next to massive cakes, shooting clay pigeons, and driving through flaming hoops on an ATK.

XP BOOST

Make sure to play with your friends if they have a Battle Pass as playing together will give you a nice XP boost. With a few of you together, it's much faster to unlock those must-have items!

COMET

2

Season 3 had just given us the chance to live out dreams as heroes and villains, but it was only the start of Epic Games introducing proper themes to the seasons. The idea of space and heroic lives gave way to Season 4, which would bring so much carnage! The new season opened with a comet heading to the world of *Fortnite* and players everywhere wondered what would happen when it landed. Nobody could guess that it was heading for the center of the map, where Dusty Depot stood.

After the comet **SMASHED** into the map, the Depot became Dusty Divot and littered the area with space rocks (Hop Rocks). When using the rocks, it changed gravity around your player, making them float around when jumping. It didn't last long, but the comet brought with it a lot of new ideas and *Fortnite* was never the same again. We saw areas change and new locations appear, such as Risky Reels, and a villain base was built in Snobby Shores, which featured a giant rocket ship!

ROCKET LAUNCH

After the map was devastated by falling space rocks, a countdown timer suddenly appeared on TV screens everywhere. But no one knew what it was counting down to. A siren began blaring from the villain's lair and the 72-hour countdown dramatically came to an end! As it did, the rocket in Snobby Shores took off and tore a rift open in the sky. Players everywhere stopped fighting and watched as chaos began. Some built ramps to try and get higher, while others sneakily destroyed the ramps to grab a huge number of kills! It was such a huge moment that most people just stood and watched in wonder.

The event was **MASSIVE,** and many websites and magazines reported on the launch of the rocket. Before this, large events generally took place off-screen, but the rocket launched in real-time over thousands of servers for people to watch.

RIFTS

The rifts appeared across the map soon after the rocket launched and managed to crack the sky. Popping up in random places, the small fractures in time and space let players fall from the sky and pull out their glider to change position or tactics. It wasn't long before the rifts began to vanish, however, and they were placed inside bottles to use whenever you felt like you needed to escape quickly or get rid of an enemy with a well-placed throw! A big downside to the rifts is the **NOISE** they make when you appear, as suddenly everyone with a sniper rifle turns in your direction and tries to pick you out of the sky.

RIFT TACTICS

The rifts are one of the most important items for tactics. Using them to change position or even just move around behind another player can change the whole match!

125 MILLION PLAYERS

After just two weeks, *Fortnite* had around 10 million players and many people wondered where the success had come from and if it would last. Little did they know that new players wouldn't stop arriving. Now you can play *Fortnite* on practically everything and this brought new players with it—the Nintendo Switch and Mobile versions made the player base much larger. In fact, the Switch version had two million players in the first day!

In June 2018 *Fortnite* had logged over 125 million players! It helps that the game is "Free-to-Play", but much of the success could be because it's easy to watch. Gamers everywhere are sharing clips and videos online! Kids and adults all have their favorite streamer, who makes them want to play even more. Watch this space as the game continues to grow.

THE BLOCK

6

What started as a totally obscure but intriguing square of concrete has quickly become one of the most innovative additions to the game yet. Located on the north east of the map at coordinates H2-H3, The Block completely flattened the old Risky Reels location! At first it was nothing more than a huge grey square, but now it is an ever-changing venue for the greatest user-generated builds from Creative Mode!

There are a few rules to follow for a creation to be considered for inclusion, but essentially anyone's could appear next! Competition to be included will be as fierce as Battle Royale itself, so if you think your creation is truly original, exciting and full of imagination then head, to Epic's website to find out how to submit it.

DID YOU KNOW?

If your creation is lucky enough to be chosen for The Block then, not only will millions of players see your work in-game, but you'll also get a shout-out on *Fortnite's* social media channels. Epic!

VEHICLES

Some Battle Royale games already had vehicles, so you might think that *Fortnite* was a little slow to react. However, in true *Fortnite* style, the first vehicle wasn't a car or a bike, but a shopping cart. There was nothing funnier than seeing a duo wheel downhill in a shopping cart–one sat inside while the other hung off the back. After this the All-Terrain Kart appeared and allowed four players to speed around the map in a fury of fire! Some Limited Time Modes also featured the jetpack, a limited time item that totally reinvented freedom of movement and your gameplay options!

And then things got **SERIOUS.** Season 6 introduced the Quadcrasher–pretty much a quad bike with a rocket engine and a blade on the front–before Season 7 took things higher and faster than ever before. The X-4 Stormwing is a five-seater fighter plane with a mounted machine gun, which, when exited, sends you back into a skydive!

GIANT CUBE (KEVIN)

One day we logged into *Fortnite* and suddenly there was a large purple cube sitting in Paradise Palms. Players poked and prodded the surface finding it springy to the touch. It was an odd appearance and players found that gliding onto the top of it would fire you back into the air. Then over the following days it began to move. The community rallied together and decided to name the cube "Kevin" and many came to play each day to see where Kevin was going. It turned out, the big purple cube was heading towards Loot Lake where it would cause even more chaos than we could imagine.

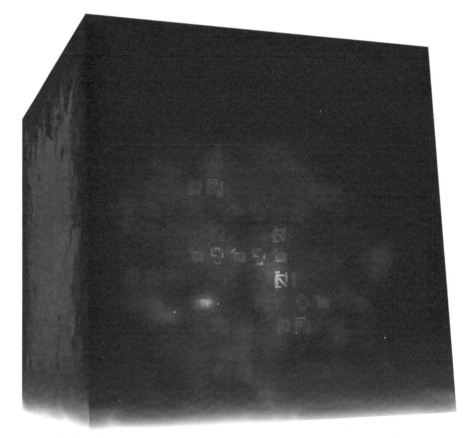

On its way to Loot Lake, Kevin kept burning purple runes into the ground as it moved, and the runes continued to spread throughout the game after it reached the lake and turned everything on its head. This was definitely one of the weirdest *Fortnite* moments yet!

LOOT LAKE CHAOS

As Season 5 came to an end and Kevin the cube arrived at Loot Lake, it slowly sunk into the depths of the waters. Everyone swarmed to the lake and found the water was now purple and bouncy! Great battles were fought while teams leaped about like bunnies. Then Season 6 took off, literally. The island in the middle of Loot Lake began to float, creating a huge storm underneath. The water lost its bounce and color and was renamed Leaky Lake, as the island began to travel west across the map. It seemed like every day something changed on the map. If you took a few days off from playing, you might find your favorite spot was no longer there, or completely different! These changes really push the idea that *Fortnite* is forever evolving.

ZIPLINES

While the arrival of Season 7 left the community discussing the snow-covered zones and the X-4 Stormwing plane, there was another change that drastically changed the way you could move around the map—without using a vehicle. Suddenly, long wires appeared, usually stretching between locations. Some went from ground level to the top of mountains, while others went from peak to peak!

By walking into the zipline you automatically start travelling along it until you reach the other side. It's best used to travel quickly around the map, to reach unlooted areas on high plateaus, or to quickly evade an enemy—but it can also save your bacon when the storm closes in on you! Just don't try and use one when you've got balloons on your back ... they'll pop!

DID YOU KNOW?

Ziplines are fast but they can draw attention to your location. You can dismount the ride at any time, so if you receive incoming fire then consider jumping off. But be warned, if you're high then the drop will cause damage.

GOODBYE

In this book, we've looked at how to be a better builder, as well as how you can be a great member of a *Fortnite* team. We explored the LTM modes and took some time to show off skins and emotes that will make you stand out on the battlefield.

We hope that the tips and information carry you to more Victory Royales!

Remember, *Fortnite* is a game and it's there for fun. As long as you try your best, play respectfully with everyone you meet and focus on learning and exploring, you'll have fun even when you aren't winning.

Fortnite holds so much—it's a huge game—so get out there, try out different modes and new guns and earn as much XP as you can from your Battle Pass.

We can't wait to see what the future brings in *Fortnite*'s exciting, ever-evolving world! See you next time, on the Battle Bus!

**The 100% UNOFFICIAL FORTNITE
PRO GUIDE team**

SAFETY TIPS

YOUNGER FANS' GUIDE

Spending time online is great fun. As *Fortnite* might be your first experience of digital socializing, here are a few simple rules to help you stay safe and keep the internet an awesome place to spend time:
• Never give out your real name—don't use it as your username.
• Never give out any of your personal details.
• Never tell anybody which school you go to or how old you are.
• Never tell anybody your password, except a parent or guardian.
• Before registering with *Fortnite*, ask a parent or guardian for permission.
• Take regular breaks, as well as playing with parents nearby, or in shared family rooms.
• Always tell a parent or guardian if something is worrying you.

> **NOTE**
> *Fortnite: Battle Royale* is ESRB rated T

PARENTS' GUIDE

ONLINE CHAT

In *Fortnite*, there is live, unmoderated voice and on-screen text chat between users. At the time of writing, turning off text chat isn't possible. You can, however, turn off voice chat:
• Open the Settings menu in the top right of the main *Fortnite* page, then the cog icon. Choose the Audio tab at the top of the screen. From there, you can adjust several audio features, including voice chat. Turn the setting from "on" to "off" by tapping the arrows.
• On consoles, you are also able to disable voice chat completely in the Parental Controls, or you can set it so your child can only chat with users who have previously been added as friends. It's important to stress to your child that they shouldn't add anyone as a friend they don't know in real life. To find these controls, see opposite about in-game purchases.

SOCIAL MEDIA SCAMS

There are many accounts on Facebook and Twitter that claim to give away free V-Bucks, which will be transferred to their account. Be sceptical—it's important to check the authenticity of these accounts and offers before giving away personal information.

SOUND

Fortnite is a game where sound is crucial. Players will often wear headphones, meaning parents won't be able to hear what is being said by strangers. Set up your console or computer to have sound coming from the TV as well as the headset so you can hear what other players are saying to your child.

REPORTING PLAYERS

If you see or hear a player being abusive, you can easily report them.
• Open the Settings menu in the main *Fortnite* page. Select the Feedback option, which allows you to report bugs, send comments or report players.
• After you've been eliminated from a game, you're also given an option to report a player by holding down the corresponding button at the bottom of the screen.

SCREEN TIME

Taking regular breaks is important. Set play sessions by using a timer. However, *Fortnite* games can last up to 20 minutes and if your child finishes playing in the middle of a round, they'll leave their teammates a person short and lose any points they've earned. So, it is advisable to give an advanced warning for stopping play.

IN-GAME PURCHASES

Fortnite does offer the ability to make in-game purchases such as new clothes, dances (emotes) and equipment, but they're not required to play the game. They also don't improve a player's performance.

To set up parental controls:
• For PlayStation 4, you can create special child accounts that can be linked to your adult account, which lets you set monthly spending limits. Log into your main PS4 account. Go to Settings > Parental Controls > Family Management. Choose Add Family Member > Create User, and then enter your child's name and date of birth. You can set up specific parental controls.

• For Xbox One, you can create a special passcode to verify purchases. Go to All Settings > Accounts > Sign-in. Then choose Change My Sign-In & Security Preferences, and scroll right to Customise. Scroll right again and select Ask For My Passkey To Make Purchases, and choose Passkey Required. Simply pick a PIN your child won't guess.

• For PC and Mac, go into the account settings of your child's Epic Games account. Once in there, make sure there aren't any card details or linked PayPal accounts. You can easily remove them if they are there.

• For iPhone and iPad, whenever you make a purchase, you'll always have to verify it with either a password, the Touch ID fingerprint scanner or Face ID. But some iPhones are set up so that you only have to enter a password every 15 minutes. To stop this, go to Settings > Your Name > iTunes & App Store. Underneath you'll see a Password Settings Section. Go to Purchases And In-App Purchases, and choose Always Require. If your child knows your iPhone password, you can set up a second PIN for purchases. Go to Settings > General > Restrictions, then press Enable Restrictions. Choose a new four-digit passcode for In-App Purchases.